Are You a Follower of Christ

Are You a Follower of Christ

Discover True Salvation

Bill Vincent

Are You a Follower of Jesus Christ
Copyright © 2014 by Bill Vincent. All rights reserved.

No part of this publication may be reproduced, stored in a retrieval system or transmitted in any way by any means, electronic, mechanical, photocopy, recording or otherwise without the prior permission of the author except as provided by USA copyright law.

Published By
Revival Waves of Glory Books & Publishing
PO Box 596
Litchfield, IL 62056

Revival Waves of Glory Books & Publishing is committed to excellence in the publishing industry.

Published in the United States of America

eBook: 978-1-312-58690-1
Paperback: 978-0692534755
Hardcover: 978-1-312-58688-8

REL012120 RELIGION / Christian Life / Spiritual Growth
REL108010 RELIGION / Christian Church / Growth
REL012070 RELIGION / Christian Life / Personal Growth

Table of Contents

Introduction 7
Midnight Hour 9
Fanning the Flame 11
Paying the Price 15
Churched 17
Becoming a Real Follower 19
About the Author 29
Recommended Books 31

Introduction

I'm burning with the word. The fire of God is going to fall. I want to tell you that any revival where there is no gospel preached, is no revival at all. Are you hearing me? A gospel that is not preached is no gospel at all.

Miracles are God's key to salvation. When God does miracles it means that people are ready to give their lives to Jesus Christ and that's what's going to happen.

You know revival has really blown my schedule out of the window. I don't have any schedule anymore. I tell you Jesus, I tell you I believe that this is only the beginning, it's only a drop in the ocean of what God has planned, if we'll just give Him the glory, if we'll just honour him and tell him its all about Him and its not about us, then I believe this could touch the world in Jesus name.

I want to release to you a message that I call Are You a Follower of Christ. Are you a follower? The bible says in Matthew 25:1, then the kingdom of heaven shall be liken to 10 virgins who took their lamps and went out to meet the bridegroom. At midnight a cry was heard: behold the bridegroom is coming. Go out to meet him.

Midnight Hour

My friend I don't know where you're from, I don't know your background, I don't know your social standing. I want to tell you, it doesn't matter who you are, I want to tell you you're living in an hour that is so close to the return of Jesus Christ. Revival is not an injection in the arm of the church just to keep them going a little bit longer. Revival is a sign that we are living in the end times, its midnight, its midnight.

I want to tell there is coming an hour where Jesus said, it shall be darkness when no man should work. I want to tell you it's midnight spiritually, it's midnight politically, it's midnight economically. We are on the doorsteps to the return of the King of Kings and Lord of Lords.

Fanning the Flame

I believe revival has been planned before the foundations of the world were even thought about. I believe that the Lord has destined moves of God that He might rescue men and women from the grip of hell. I thank God for every healing, every miracle, but one of the greatest miracle of all is when a man or a woman bows their knee to Jesus Christ.

I wasn't always a preacher; I was a young man with rebellion in his heart. By the time I was 17, I was already away from church, away from God, running as fast as my legs could carry me from the cord that was on my life. There are those of you, you've grown up in church, you knew the Lord but you're no where near the call and the destiny and the path that God has ordained in your life.

You know there are people in this place but you are a follower of Jesus Christ, you're a follower of Jesus. I hear people telling me, "I'm a Christian," with a bottle larger in their hand.

There are people that are like the many of the disciples in the Bible. If you read in John 6:63, you will read this, it is the spirit. Jesus said, "It is the Spirit who gives life; the flesh profits for nothing. The words that speaker to you are spirit and they are life." There are some of you who do not believe, for Jesus knew from the beginning who the people were that did not believe and who would betray. He said, "Therefore I said to you that no one can come to me unless it has been granted to him by my father."

Now I want you to hear this church, I want to hear this to every young man, every young woman, every old man and every old woman, hear the words of this preacher right now. Jesus the bible says from that time many of His disciples went back and walked with Him no more. Many of those that had walked with Jesus, they experienced what they wanted, did the miracles whilst he set the captives free, they walked with him. There came a time in their lives where the price was just too much. They were a follower but they were never a follower. We have missed what it means to follow Christ.

I want to ask you, you may love revival, you may love the presence, you might come to watch the miracles, but are you a follower, are you truly a disciple, a follower of Jesus Christ? Are you willing to go no matter where he tells you to go? Are you willing to lay down your plans and your dreams and all that you think you have at the feet of Jesus?

Paying the Price

See many of those people who were around Jesus, they were close enough to see the good stuff; they were close enough to see the miracles and the power. When it got tough, in the moment where that word pierced their heart, they suddenly stepped aside away from the son of God. I see Christians they want to be in revival but they don't want to pay the price. The second criticism begins to come, the second hell begins to accuse, you don't see them anymore, they're gone. They were a fan of revival but they weren't a follower of Jesus Christ.

Churched

Jesus said in Matthew 15:8, "These people draw near to me with their mouth, they honour me with their lips but their heart is far from me." Their heart is far from me. When Jesus looks at you, when he looks past and the smile on your face when he looks into your heart, does he see a man or a woman that is a true follower after Jesus? Yes, you can come here, you can sing the songs, you can wave your hands, you can dance about with your heart before from Jesus. Are You a follower of Christ?

I grew up in church, I knew how church ticked. I knew who was going to pray, when they were going to pray, how long they would pray for; I knew how many songs we are going to sing. I knew who was going to be the kind of guy that danced around. I watched it all my life. Many hearts were far from Jesus.

I want to ask you a question. Do you know Him? Your people, do you know Jesus? I want to tell you some of you are playing around with things that these world and you have no idea that the chains of hell are wrapping their chains of bondage around your life. I said this many times, don't dance with the devil, he will take you under.

I want to tell you we're living in an hour where being a admirer of Jesus won't cut the mustard. You're not going to make it. There's coming an hour when God will pull out of His Glory but the darkness in this world will be so dark that being just a admirer will never make it through the night hour. Behold the bridegroom cometh. Half of them didn't have any oil in their lamps to make it through the night. They were admirers of Jesus, they carried the name of Jesus but their heart was far from him.

There's an hour where men will say, "Jesus, did we not cast out devils in your name?" The bible says that Jesus will walk from his throne with eyes of fire. His glory will pierce your heart and he will say, "Go from me. I never knew you."

"You may say I did not come to get depressed." Listen, I don't care how you feel. I've come that your soul is not damned in hell.

Becoming a Real Follower

I want to talk about Peter. I want to talk about a disciple, the bold disciple Peter, the guy that when Jesus asked the question, "Who do the they say I am?" He was the one that had the revelation, "You're the Christ, the son of the living God." Peter the one that looked to Jesus in the storm, he looked at Christ and he said, "If you just bid me come, I'll walk on the water."

Some of you are on fire for God. You're burning for God. You do whatever Jesus told you to do. You are willing to lay down your life; you're willing to do all the things that God required of you. You're dead, there's no fire in you, there's no passion in you. You're banished to sin to the things of this world.

See the Bible says that Jesus said to Peter, "Peter, Satan has asked that he may sift you as wheat." This disciple that had walked with Jesus, that had walked and seen the miracles, these bold disciple suddenly Satan said that he would take him out.

I want to tell those of you, some of you have had hard lives, some of you have not known the love of the father. Some may be here that have been abused. Satan, from the moment you entered this world has sought to sift you, to cripple you, to grab you in bitterness and pain. He can see that God has a plan for your life.

The Bible says when Jesus was being laid to the cross, when the Son of God was about to take on the sins of this world, he was about to hang on the cross, beaten so badly he was unrecognizable. They had opened up his back until the bible says that his back was like a plough field. I want to tell you Jesus wasn't a admirer of you; He was a lover of your soul. When it was His moment to step up to the plan for you, He never backed down, He never batted an eyelid, He stepped up there and faced hell head on.

Satan came to sift him, Satan came to profit him, to tempt him, but Jesus when He saw you, when He looked at you, He wasn't a admirer of you, He was a lover of your soul.

When Jesus was going to stand before Pilate, the gospel is going to preach to me, something that God has put in my heart. As I preach, I've seen the fire of this message break every chain that Satan has longed to hold you down with. As Jesus was going to stand before Pilate, the bible says that Peter his disciple, this man that was going to be a follower of Christ, the Bible says that he distanced himself from Christ and he was warming himself by the fire.

Some of you, you're on fire for God, you have a passion for souls and then satan began to draw you that you might warm yourself in the fires of this world. I see preachers, the ones that have passion to see souls saved and then Satan came with the money and with the riches and with the fame. He said, "Warm yourself, warm yourself by the fires of this world." If he would have only looked at it, the saviour, if he only were to look at the eyes of his saviour, I know that he would have known in that moment Satan was sifting his soul.

Satan will lure you until you don't see Jesus anymore, until you're warm in yourself by the fire and suddenly he tests you. "Aren't you that man, aren't you that follower of Christ?" The bible says that Peter, this man that said to have been calm, he so distanced himself, he was warming himself by the fire and he denied Christ.

I don't know where you are, but I know I'm strong at the life line. The hour is late, don't play, don't gamble with your soul.

Jesus! Peter denied Christ, but what I love, I know when Jesus sat on the cross, I know that when the blood dripped from his side, when the father had turned his face in that moment that Jesus hang there, I know that He saw Peter. I know that He knew Peter had denied Him. I know is that blood shed on the cross and that blood dripped from his side, he knew not what Peter was but what he would become. He knew this admirer of Jesus was going to become a follower and he would lay down his life for the kingdom of God.

What I love is Jesus comes to find, He died, He rose again. The Bible says that even He went into heavens, He went down to hell, He took the keys of death and of hell and He rose victorious. What I love is that the love of God He came looking for Peter, he wouldn't leave Him because He knew that this admirer would one day be his follower, a disciple that would have a passion to preach Pentecost.

God, is calling those of you back to the passion, back to the fall, back to Himself. My Lord, I feel this so strong. I love what Jesus said to Peter. Jesus said to him, "Peter, do you love me? Do you love me?" What he was really saying was, "Peter, are you a admirer?" You might sing the songs, but is your heart rendered on to me?

Jesus used the word called agape; it means a very special and deep kind of love. It means you will love with your heart. How long will you run from God? How long are you going to run from the saviour? Young people, to my friends, to my friends that I went to school with, to my friends that if they saw me, ever get saved, I would preach to them.

While your love goes cold, the enemy laughs over you. Jesus looks at Peter, He looks in the eyes and He says, "Peter, do you like me? Do you like me?" Peter said, "Yes."

You maybe sat in your seat and you might have been in church more years than I have been born. I'm not asking you to hear my words. I'm asking you to look in the presence of God and your heart and say, "God, am I on fire? Am I burning with the passion of the gospel? Lord am I admirer or am I truly a disciple of God?"

Let me tell you, you might be asking God for miracles in your life but God is asking you tonight, would you lay down your life and let me breathe upon you again?

Jesus said, "Whoever desires to come after me, let him deny himself, let him take up his cross, let me follow me. For whoever desires to save his life, he will lose it." You might be trying to hold on to these things that you lead upon in your life but you don't realize you will loose your soul in the process. Let go, let go. Let Jesus breath in your life.

What I love about Peter is when Pentecost hits, the fire of God falls on him. This man that I had denied, this man that was a admirer suddenly he had an encounter with the fire of the Holy Ghost. The power God invaded his life and suddenly this man was changed from a fan into a disciple of Jesus Christ.

I want to tell you, no counselling cost, no seven steps to the eight ways of the nine points. Only the blood that was shed from the Lamb of God has the power to make you a new creation.

When the fire of God hit me, everything went out of the window. I said, "Lord I don't care, just set me on fire that I may burn for you. Set me on fire that I may burn for you.

Lord I don't want to be a pew filler, I want to be a tongue speaking, lay hands on the sick and they shall recover. I want to preach the gospel of the son of God that died to take away the sins of this world. Are you a follower? What's your price? What has Satan offered you that you took it hard line and sinker? What does he offer you that has drawn you to warm yourself against the fires of this world? Is it a man? Is it a woman? Is it a business deal? Well Jesus, I know that they're corrupt; I know that they're deceitful, but Jesus, I want that money, you know that I will give it to the kingdom. That is filthy money that will damn your soul. Get your hands off it, stop woving your hands from what the enemy will give you. Jesus shall supply all your of your needs.

Look at what peter said in three lines, follow me and he will watch you, he will cleanse you, he will set you on fire. You won't be the same, you won't walk the same, you won't talk the same, you will be baptised in the Holy Ghost and fire.

Many of you tonight are in your seat and your heart tum tum tum; you know it, tum, tum, tum. When the fire of God fell on me, I had drug habits.

The Bible says that God won't always strife with you, he wont always strife with your rebellion. One day you're going to ask to give an account of what you did with the author that God made you.

God's Altar is always open. The power of God is going to break out, the same power that brings crippled people out of wheelchairs, the same power that opens the eye of the blind, is the same spirit that tonight is going to raise you out of the deadness of your sin and raise you up to be a saint of the living God. Some of you are going to walk from this place still wearing the mask, some of you are going to walk from this place criticising the Bible. Some of you are going to walk from this place in chains of the devil because you know that you know that God is dealing with your heart.

I've got enough sense to say this, don't fight with God, you're going to lose. You're going to lose. Whom the son sets free is free indeed. Set you free all over this place quickly. Its time to get right with Jesus.

About the Author

Bill Vincent is an Apostle and Author with Revival Waves of Glory Ministries in Litchfield, IL. Bill and his wife Tabitha work closely in every day ministry duties. Bill and Tabitha lead a team providing Apostolic over sight in all aspects of ministry, including service, personal ministry and Godly character.

Bill is a believer in Jesus Christ in the fullness of power with signs and wonders. Bill has an accurate prophetic gift, a powerful revelatory preaching anointing with miracles signs and wonders following.

Bill Vincent is no stranger to understanding the power of God, having spent over twenty years as a Minister with a strong prophetic anointing, which taught him the importance of deliverance by the power of God. Bill has more than thirty prophetic books available all over the world. Prior to starting his ministry, Revival Waves of Glory he spent the last few years as a Pastor of a Church and a traveling prophetic ministry.

Bill Vincent helps the Body of Christ to get closer to God while overcoming the enemy. Bill offers a wide range of writings and teachings from deliverance, to the presence of God and Apostolic cutting edge Church structure. Drawing on the power of the Holy Spirit through years of experience in Revival, Spiritual Sensitivity and deliverance ministry, Bill now focuses mainly on pursuing the Presence of God and breaking the power of the devil off of people's lives.

His book Defeating the Demonic Realm was published in 2011 and has since helped many people to overcome the spirits and curses of satan. Since then Bill's books have flooded the market with his writings released just like he prophesies the Word of the Lord.

Bill Vincent is a unique man of God whom has discovered; powerful ways to pursue God's presence, releasing revelations of the demonic realm and prophetic anointing through everything he does. Bill is always moving forward at a rapid pace and there is sure to be much more released by him in upcoming years.

Recommended Books

By Bill Vincent
Overcoming Obstacles
Glory: Pursuing God's Presence
Defeating the Demonic Realm
Increasing Your Prophetic Gift
Increase Your Anointing
Keys to Receiving Your Miracle
The Supernatural Realm
Waves of Revival
Increase of Revelation and Restoration
The Resurrection Power of God
Discerning Your Call of God
Apostolic Breakthrough
Glory: Increasing God's Presence
Love is Waiting – Don't Let Love Pass You By
The Healing Power of God
Glory: Expanding God's Presence
Receiving Personal Prophecy
Signs and Wonders
Signs and Wonders Revelations
Children Stories
The Rapture
The Secret Place of God's Power
Building a Prototype Church
Breakthrough of Spiritual Strongholds
Glory: Revival Presence of God
Overcoming the Power of Lust
Glory: Kingdom Presence of God
Transitioning to the Prototype Church
The Stronghold of Jezebel
Healing After Divorce

A Closer Relationship With God
Cover Up and Save Yourself
Desperate for God's Presence
The War for Spiritual Battles
Spiritual Leadership
Global Warning
Millions of Churches
Destroying the Jezebel Spirit
Awakening of Miracles
Deception and Consequences Revealed
Are You a Follower of Christ
Don't Let the Enemy Steal from You!
A Godly Shaking
The Unsearchable Riches of Christ
Heaven's Court System
Satan's Open Doors
Armed for Battle
The Wrestler
Spiritual Warfare: Complete Collection
Growing In the Prophetic
The Prototype Church: Complete Edition
Faith
The Angry Fighter's Story
Understanding Heaven's Court System

Web Site:
www.revivalwavesofgloryministries.com

www.ingramcontent.com/pod-product-compliance
Lightning Source LLC
Chambersburg PA
CBHW052000290426
44110CB00015B/2315